Six-Word Lessons to

OVERCOME ABUSE

AND ADVERSITY

100 Lessons to Courageously
Move Forward Using
Forward Principles

Rae Ann Hall

Published by Pacelli Publishing
Bellevue, Washington

Six-Word Lessons to Overcome Abuse and Adversity

Published by Pacelli Publishing
9905 Lake Washington Blvd. NE, #D-103
Bellevue, Washington 98004
PacelliPublishing.com

Cover and interior designed by Pacelli Publishing
Author photo by Kercheval Photography, Lake Forest Park, WA
Cover image by iStock.com/RapidEye

ISBN-10: 1-933750-79-0
ISBN-13: 978-1-933750-79-8

Dedication

To my brother and sister who pulled me out of darkness, and to the Savior whose light and strength gave me true healing. To my husband and precious girl who give depth and meaning to my life and a true sense of fulfillment.

Life is a collaborative effort. We embrace the good and work through the bad together because together we are stronger than we are on our own.

Table of Contents

"Pain nourishes courage. You can't be brave if you've only had wonderful things happen to you."
--Mary Tyler Moore

Introduction

As a child I was sexually abused on a continual basis for many years. As an adult I attracted similar abuse patterns in relationships until I intentionally changed my beliefs about my own worth, core values, and life's possibilities, and lived my life on purpose. The inspiration for this book is to share *Forward Principles* which helped me and others through the rough times in life and continue to help press forward in a positive way.

The effects of abuse go on throughout life, and it takes a little extra effort to forge ahead, especially when others around you do not understand the down days or the long-term effects of abuse survivors. As survivors, we learn to face this world as if nothing happened, so we can "fit in" and live a somewhat normal life. Many keep silent, afraid of the stigma that comes from being a victim of abuse. Yet something did happen, and something was taken from us. However, we can heal and move forward, making it through the aftermath and forging ahead in hope for the present and future. We can stand in our truth, letting go of shame and embracing our innate gifts given to us to move through this life in happiness and peace.

This book is filled with positivity which helps combat the negativity and darkness that can unfortunately be a part of this life. It can come in many different forms. Whether it is abusive relationships, financial hardship, healing from sickness, loss of a loved one, work challenges, or day-to-day relationships, these principles will help you get centered and move forward in a positive, healthy way. They helped me move forward intentionally through many situations and have helped my friends through rough times as well.

Explaining *Forward Principles*

FORWARD PRINCIPLES is my terminology for the practical steps I have used along my journey of being an abuse survivor. They are actionable ways to intentionally move forward in a positive way. Each chapter in this book is related to a *Forward Principle*.

First: BE IN THE PRESENT

This is about getting into the present with what happened, and not suppressing or burying it.

Second: INTENTIONALLY FACE EACH DAY

Life doesn't stop, so you need to intentionally face each day with extra effort to get through because you will feel depleted if you are not filling yourself up and planning with focus.

Third: SOURCE OF LIGHT AND STRENGTH

Fill yourself with your source of strength and light to replenish and gain momentum.

Fourth: BE ACCOUNTABLE

Pull yourself out of victim mode by being accountable for your actions today and how you move forward. This helps change your mindset and the trap that can come by staying focused on the injustice of what happened. You need to move forward intentionally and even strategically.

Fifth: RESILIENCE MENTALITY

Resilience is key. You are going to have ups and downs. We all do; it's a part of life. Surviving abuse, especially in your younger years, has long-term effects. Facing the setbacks or dark memories and getting back up is key for gaining continued inner strength and maintaining a positive self-image. Seek help and implement the advice you are getting, using your wisdom while still being challenged to embrace new ideas that will break limiting beliefs.

Sixth: EMBRACE YOUR UNIQUE SELF

Embrace who you are, good and bad, be authentic and claim your unique brilliance.

Seventh: WISELY CHOOSE SUPPORT

Seek help, implementing advice wisely. Utilize support groups, leaning on people who relate to what you have gone through.

Eighth: GOALS

Forward motion includes setting goals and being clear on the desired outcome--what it will take.

Ninth: EMBRACE FEELING OF SUCCESS

As you start to see success and be filled with hope and a sense of well-being, sometimes it can feel foreign; especially if you have been in disarray for awhile (it can begin to feel more normal being in a state of chaos). It is so important to claim the new feeling that comes from intentionally moving forward and achieving goals, embracing the light and your successes. You want to move forward from the pain and gain confidence in your purpose.

Tenth: SERVICE AND GIVING BACK

Giving back and serving helps you feel better and keeps you out of your own mind. It is also sharing your strength and wisdom that brings good from the bad, leaving you with a meaningful feeling inside, and a sense of fulfillment.

Accept Where You Are Right Now

1

Be present where you are now.

An important thing needs to happen before you can move forward in a healthy way: you need to accept what has happened and be in the present. Throughout this book, there will be simple yet impactful tools (*Forward Principles*) that will help you work through the emotions of this adversity. The focus will be what you can do going forward, healing the pain and filling the void you may feel inside, regaining strength.

2

Breathe in the possibility of forgiveness.

Forgiveness is a journey, but a worthy process which enables you to release the burden of bitter feelings. You stunt yourself when you let bitterness consume you. You can be imprisoned by the negative effects of holding a grudge. Breathe in new life, let go of bitterness, forgive the person, not the act. Repeat this process when anger and bitterness return. You will reach peace with this through continued effort.

3

Breathe out negative and limiting beliefs.

Breathing techniques will be beneficial in letting go of negative feelings and even limiting beliefs. As you breathe in deeply, think of new life, hope and light, visualizing your best life. As you exhale, visualize the release of the tension and negative energy. Let go of limiting beliefs that bind you down. It works! Release, replace, repeat.

4

Know the past doesn't define you.

Claiming where you are right now and being present with what has happened in no way means you are stuck here, in this pain. What happened to you does not define you, how you move forward does. This is part of your journey and as you push forward, you will inspire others to do the same. You will be liberated when you see your potential and live your purpose.

5

How you move forward cultivates hope.

As you do things to feed your spirit and work toward your peaceful life, you will begin feeling more and more hope. Embrace the hope that comes when you decide to not stay stuck in someone else's misery. Their darkness brought pain and darkness, but you do not have to be stuck there. You can embrace light and be filled with hope for healing and fulfillment.

6

Build on hope to cultivate belief.

Being filled with hope will cultivate a more positive outlook. You will begin to build more belief in yourself and the good in the world. You will begin to believe that brighter days will come, and that your life has meaning and purpose.

7

Turn belief into passion for present.

The momentum of hope and belief will begin to fill you with passion. Especially as you see your best life in sight and are pushing forward. The present day begins to be lived on purpose with intention and clarity. Fuel that passion into your daily activities and you will grow exponentially.

8

Embrace light when dark memories come.

Overcoming adversity is a process. Bad memories may come, and the darkness will try to creep back into your life. Embrace light and envision it filling your soul. Turn to your source of light and hope and don't give in to the darkness that can feel overwhelming. Believe you will get through this moment. It will take extra effort, but it's a worthy fight to not give into the darkness.

9

Forgiveness is key in moving forward.

You can approach forgiveness again, especially after being reminded that dark memories may come. Remember the process and that forgiveness is a journey. For you to feel at peace and be released of anger and hate toward the awful thing that happened, and it is awful, forgive so you can be set free. Forgiving the person isn't keeping them in your life. Forgive, move on and keep safe boundaries.

10

Envision possibility of a positive future.

What you think about, comes about. The mind can achieve what it sees. Take time to envision what is possible, what will be, what can be, and what good you will do. Envision the right people coming into place to put things in motion for you to live your purpose and passion. Your vision and how you see yourself, even the future, is what ignites it coming into fruition.

Intentionally Go Through Each Day Consistently

11

Begin your day in strength intentionally.

How you start your day will set the tone for the day. Begin the day intentionally, tapping into what gives you the most strength and fills you up inside. This will give you more energy that you will use giving to others and to projects. You can't give what isn't in you. When overcoming hardships, you can feel very depleted inside. Nurturing yourself and filling up with extra strength will help you stay on course and make it through.

12

Each day is a growing opportunity.

Good and bad things come up throughout the day, but develop the attitude that they are learning experiences to keep growing. Set the tone for the day, make the best choices you can, be intentional on your tasks, but know that things are going to happen. These things will be different each day and facing them will prepare you for future opportunities, even dealing with situations that may come up again.

13

Focus on your day with purpose.

Take time to plan your day with focus. Start with your purpose, being clear on who you are and what you can accomplish (mindset). Write out all the tasks you need to complete and number or code them in order of importance and priority. Keep it simple but intentional. You will accomplish more with clear intention, setting priorities and believing in yourself—tapping into your purpose.

14

Decide how to face setbacks now.

As the bumps in the day come, and they usually do, adjust and move forward. When you decide ahead of time how you will respond in those moments, you will handle it much better. Some days are smooth, and others have surprises. Either way, decide now how you will respond, and what you will do to not let it distract or destroy your purpose and priorities.

15

Each day builds on your strength.

As the days move on, after a traumatic experience or adversity, time will be your friend. Especially if used productively with intention. At first the days may be harder to get through, but as you build on each day applying these principles and keep moving forward, you will continue to get more strength which will develop even more strength.

16

Be flexible without giving up purpose.

If you have important things as well as occasional family emergencies that come up during the day, of course you will be flexible and move those up the priority list. Keep your focus and purpose, rearranging what you can so you stay on task and in integrity. You will find the solution. Be careful not to let other people's lack of preparation become an emergency for you.

17

Reflect on what went right today.

A great way to continue building confidence, hope and inner strength is to reflect daily on your wins. Take time to appreciate all the good that came into your life every day and how you handled any setbacks. Celebrate the strength and progress you see in yourself. Journal your strength attributes on display each day and the great things you accomplished.

18

Stretch, relax and journal your day.

A great way to unwind from the day is to do stretching exercises; it clears your body of tensions and your mind of stress. Journaling your wins, activities, insights and thoughts of the day is a great way to keep you moving forward, building on strengths. Ending your journal entry with something you are grateful for keeps the positive mental attitude and helps cultivate a positive outlook, which builds inner strength.

19

End days in love and appreciation.

Love gives you light and energy which brings healing and peace. Take a moment before your head hits the pillow to fill yourself with love and light from your source of strength, appreciating the gifts received that day. Whether that is praying, reading or meditating, you will be strengthened and find inner peace as you fill yourself with love. Self-love is a necessary component to inner peace.

20

Envision best self when closing eyes.

As you lie in bed, a great practice is to envision your best self and your best life. See yourself achieving your goals and feel what it is like to be that person in that moment of truly living your best life and fulfilling your passion. If you can see it, you can achieve it. Let it become a part of you and let your mind claim it.

Your Center of Strength and Light

21

Turn to your source of light.

What is your greatest source of light and strength? Take time to discover it. When you find what truly feeds your soul beyond your own power, tap into it often. Knowing what your center of strength is and embracing it fills your soul up with healing and light. You have everything in you to overcome, and there are resources to help you move forward. Tap into both.

22

Be firm in your belief system.

Discover what makes you feel centered and connected to your energy source. What are your core values, principles and beliefs? Discover or rediscover who you are and what motivates you. Stay true to your convictions and live by them. As you live what you believe, you will have integrity and attract good things to you. Inner peace, stability and strength come from living in alignment with your core beliefs.

23

Find inner strength through daily meditation.

Take time to meditate and be one with your thoughts, connecting to enlightenment from your source of light. This is crucial in healing the scars of abuse and nurturing your soul. It will give you strength, cultivating inner peace. Meditation will help you have trust again and invite love into your heart. Walking every day and pondering on things helps your body and mind.

24

Quiet the noise in your home.

Too much noise in your home creates chaos. Quieting the noise in your home will calm your mind and help you to continue regaining your strength. Also, the wrong kind of noise in your home can bring darkness. You want to create an atmosphere in your home that is calm, fun, and filled with light. Open the shades, declutter and keep it clean. It really helps you feel better.

25

Avoid taking on another person's chaos.

Compassion and helping others is worthy; that is not what is being addressed here. Chaos is random and uninvited. If someone starts dumping their worries and anger on you, you have a choice to stay in that moment or kindly exit. Take a call, go to the bathroom, or straight up tell them you are not in a place to help them with their issues.

26

Tap into strength through breathing techniques.

Breathing techniques are great because you can do them anywhere at any time to bring down the stress level or just get recentered. Breathe in deeply, hold and then exhale; you will feel your body relax and your mind clear. You can even experience a reduction in heart rate and blood pressure when you take deep, slow breaths for ten minutes a day.

27

Remind yourself that you are worthy.

Your self-talk and belief in yourself is fundamental in overcoming the negative effects of abuse. When you take time regularly to appreciate and fully understand your great worth, you can begin to refuel your self-image, connect to your infinite worth, and get past someone using you and not respecting your mind, body and spirit. You can separate their act from your great value.

28

Kindly exit situations that contradict beliefs.

With all the work on finding your belief system and living your core values, protect them and exit situations that are taking you away from your center. In keeping your convictions and controlling your surroundings the best you can, it will help you stay connected to inner peace. You have a choice what you invite into your mind and the environment you choose to be in will protect that.

29

Find a place to quietly recenter.

Find a few places at home, work, or school where you can be with your thoughts and have quiet time. Five minutes in silence alone can recharge you from the things happening around you or the people around you. Avoid becoming drained and feeling empty by the end of the day by taking time throughout your day to breathe and get centered with your source of light.

30

Be in the moment through grounding.

When overwhelming memories or feelings come, grounding can help you work through them, bringing you back into the present moment. A Robert Frost poem says ". . . the best way out is always through." Suppressing feelings is not healthy. Find a quiet place where you can feel what you are feeling, and emotionally and logically make your way back into the present. Research grounding techniques that will work for you.

Be Accountable for Your own Actions

31

Be known for keeping your commitments.

Integrity and inner strength begin with keeping your word. You cannot control what happened, but you can control how you move forward. It is important to move out of victim mode and be accountable for your own actions moving forward in life, to gain momentum and confidence. Stay away from blaming, own who you are and live with integrity. Keeping commitments builds integrity.

32

Speak and live truth never lying.

Integrity is also speaking the truth. Inner strength and confidence in self is experienced when you are at one with your core values and living an honest life. Dishonesty tears down people, families and organizations. Believe in your worth, nothing needs to be embellished or exaggerated. You can face mistakes and own up to your part--in fact it propels you forward. Honesty cultivates trust and a guilt-free feeling.

33

Accept responsibility when you make mistakes.

Minimizing your part will keep the mistake happening. Often it is simply owning your mistake that helps you move forward and see it for what it is, a learning opportunity. Every person in this life makes mistakes. Look at the situation, see what you did wrong and own it. When you focus on what you did, you can do something about it.

34

Place the mask on yourself first.

Nurturing yourself with love and kindness fuels you to give your best and be there for friends and loved ones. Developing talents, building on your strengths, self-care and positive mental attitude take continued effort; but they all fill you up and create the type of person you want to be. They also replenish the hole that you may feel inside after the abuse or adversity.

35

What are you doing wrong now?

Self-check to stay on course. When you make mistakes, assess what might be going wrong and what decisions you are making that are leading you down the wrong path. The first step toward change and progress is acknowledgement and awareness of what might be going wrong, so you can do something about it. This isn't a beat-yourself-up moment, it's a simple assessment to lovingly course-correct.

36

What are you doing correctly now?

When self-checking, also look for all the good you are doing and the great decisions you are making. See your progress which will help you to keep building self-confidence and a positive mindset. Build on your strengths, creating what you want. When you feel good about where you are and what is going right, your outlook is good, and you do good in the world.

37

Look for your part in conflict.

Take ownership of your part in any conflict because that is all you can do something about. If the other person stays out of integrity and doesn't own their part, that is on them and you cannot change that. Focusing on the other person only puts you in victim mode. You can also lose valued friends by only seeing what they did wrong.

38

Keep your behavior in check consistently.

You decide how you are going to behave. Being consistent with your behavior develops trust in yourself, and people know you are trustworthy. Don't try for perfection, just consistent behavior in line with your morals and values. In stressful moments, utilize the grounding and breathing techniques to calm you and recenter yourself. If you find your behavior spiking out of your control, you may want to consult your doctor.

39

You control your thoughts and mindset.

Life is what you make it. You can dwell on the bad and think about all that went wrong. Or you can make a choice to turn your thoughts to pushing forward, utilizing the tools you are learning about to heal and replenish. Your thoughts about yourself and life is your mindset; take care of that and be sure to think the best of yourself and believe in yourself.

40

Your attitude is up to you.

Having a can-do attitude helps you focus on solutions and having a positive mental attitude affects your outlook on your day-to-day life. Having joy is always an option. Find the music, talks, quotes and poems that bring happiness and a spark in your attitude. Have some fun--laughter is the best medicine. Choose joy.

Be a Champion of Resilience Mentality

41

Get up when you're knocked down.

Something, someone or some situation will inevitably come that will knock you down. Process the emotions of it, let them out and think your way through. Trust your instincts and use wisdom to see your way back up. Take a break and come to terms with it; just get back up. The only time you fail is when you stop trying, so use your tools to keep you moving forward.

42

What you focus on will expand.

The way to resiliency is often found in the thoughts you focus on. If you keep focusing on the problem, it will become bigger and bigger in your mind, sometimes taking on a life of its own. Shift the focus to actions going forward and the positive things you can do to turn it around. Focus on possibilities and goals, visualizing success. Let that continue to expand.

43

Feel what you feel allowing emotion.

Again, the only way out is through. Face it, feel it and let the emotions come out. It is healing! Of course, find the right place to do this and avoid getting stuck in the emotions. But feel them, let it out and come to terms with how normal it is to feel these things. Suppressing your feelings will eat away at you.

44

Use logic to bring back sanity.

After the emotions are processed and expressed, use logic to bring you back to the present. It can be overwhelming, especially the closer you are to the incident or adversity, but if you express the emotion and use logic to move forward it will get easier with time and the emotions will come less often because you are healing.

45

See what you learned from it.

Another way of being resilient in a healthy way is seeing all that you learned from the situation. Taking time to appreciate the growth can help you bounce back and even be a better person. It may not seem that way in the middle of the trauma, but eventually you will start to see what you learned and the good that can come from something so unfortunate.

46

Remember when you succeeded at overcoming.

When you draw upon past successes to help overcome the tough times, you can see that you have what it takes to make it through. You can approach it with confidence and draw on the strength inside. Remember what worked and visualize yourself coming through the trial.

47

You keep fighting the worthy fight.

This is a worthy fight, and at times it will feel like a fight against other forces trying to knock you down or even keep you down. Keep fighting for your life, your emotional wellbeing and the light that will come. You deserve a happy life and will achieve it by not giving up. Be determined, you are worth it. REMEMBER, you are worth it!

48

You are important and have purpose.

When you are experiencing a down day or in a slump, tap into your purpose, even if it is a slight glimmer that you see. Feed your thoughts with your passions and potential. Feel how loved you are and know you are important. It will help you get back up and keep trying when you remember your infinite worth and start fueling yourself with your passion again.

49

This adversity can make you stronger.

This adversity will most likely become a catalyst to make you even stronger. When you come through the fire of the trial and look back, you will see that you are indeed stronger. Approach this trial with assurance, reminding yourself that it is part of your growing process and is making you stronger because you are facing it and using your tools to push forward.

50

Experiences endured prepare for future opportunities.

The growing lessons of your experience and what you have endured will be a blessing for someone else or even yourself to draw on in the future. You have purpose and you have everything in you to endure this trial to face what needs to be faced. It shifts your mindset when you see purpose for the trial and helps you face it better. Believe this will be triumphed and that good will come of it.

Embrace Your Differences and Unique Self

51

Own your quirks and understand weaknesses.

Own your quirks and unique personality. It is freeing, and you attract more into your life. People love an authentic person. Avoid measuring yourself based on your weaknesses but understand what they are. It can help you be wise when making commitments. Know that those weaknesses can even become strengths one day, just be in the moment and be real with where you are now.

52

Make a list of your strengths.

Take your time and develop a list of all your wonderful strengths. Exhaust all your efforts to see every possible strength you have seen in yourself, as well as those that others have seen in you. Remember your successes and attributes that helped you achieve each success. Listing all your strengths helps you see all you have to work with and contributes to good self-esteem.

53

Take personality test building on talents.

Personality tests are great resources to draw out your strengths and talents. A personality test can help reveal your strengths and how to use them for your personal growth and to live out your purpose. A good comprehensive test to start with can be found at GallupStrengthCenter.com. Your results will outline how to build on your strengths, develop your talents, and live your best life.

54

Look in mirror talking to yourself.

This might be uncomfortable at first, but you are the person you will be with the rest of your life. Give yourself love and pep talks. Be comfortable encouraging yourself and believing in yourself, because that is how you are going to succeed. Take a minute to see you, believe in your abilities and claim your purpose so you can live it. Be your biggest ally and best friend.

55

It is healthy to love yourself.

What you feel about yourself exudes to others whether you realize it or not. When you have a love for yourself and a healthy respect for who you are, you hold your head high and have a positive outlook and others will respond to that. You show people how to treat you by the way you see yourself. It is healthy to love yourself and be at peace with who you are.

56

Have alone times for inner strength.

Taking time to fill yourself up with strength will be important. Even five minutes alone can keep you centered and fill your inner strength. Time alone, away from the hectic things that may be going on around you, will help you stay focused and not get pulled into any chaos. Nurturing yourself is a way to sort through things, to get connected with your strengths and forge ahead.

57

Write about ideas and your passion.

Writing about your ideas and passion will fuel more passion and build on your dreams. Thinking about what things you would like to do or try and how you could achieve them is great, and putting them on paper helps you give birth to the ideas and bring them to life. It ignites more enthusiasm and builds on your ideas, even making your dreams bigger as you put things in motion; acting them out.

58

Find what brings you true joy.

When have you felt true joy and happiness? Not the happiness that goes away the next day, but the happiness that fills your soul and gives you true joy. As you discover all the things that bring you that fulfilling sense of joy, be sure to take time to bring more of those things into your life. Life is meant to be enjoyed; bring back the laughter and lighten things up.

59

Nurture yourself with what gives energy.

Filling your soul with energy is key in healing and replenishing. Think about what brings that in your life--prayer, reading, meditating, walking, being in nature? Who are you around, what are your surroundings and activities when you are feeling your best and getting fed emotionally? Tap into what gives you strength and energy often; it keeps you moving forward in a healthy way.

60

Say affirmations every morning and believe.

Affirmations are positive statements about yourself; a way to reprogram any limiting beliefs. They help you to stay positive and focus on your goals, even programming your subconscious mind, i.e., "I am healthy," "I am driven," etc. Say or write down your affirmations each morning, believing in yourself and the things coming your way. This contributes to a positive self-image and helps you build on your strengths.

Seek Help and Implement Advice Wisely

61

Focused support groups can be helpful.

Support groups can be great. Find one that fills you up inside. Identifying with other people who have been through similar trials is so strengthening. It is helpful to know that you are not alone; you will feel less isolated. Speaking your thoughts and things you are going through in a safe environment with people who have true empathy for you is very healing.

62

Try therapists until one gets you.

Therapists are great and each one has something to offer. You can ask people in your support group for recommendations or look up therapists close to you who may even specialize in your situation. It is definitely O.K. to try a couple of them out before making a commitment to stick with one. The important thing is that you feel understood, and that they challenge you to move forward.

63

Be around those who give strength.

Be selective on choosing your inner circle of friends and associates. Protect yourself the best you can with a positive environment and a supportive network. Charlie "Tremendous" Jones said, "You are the same today that you are going to be five years from now except for two things: the people with whom you associate and the books you read."

64

Ponder on advice, follow with wisdom.

Apply the things you are learning and the advice you are getting with wisdom. Using your intellect and wisdom to implement the things that make sense and challenge you is an important component to growth. Never blindly follow, but seek out the wisdom, ponder and meditate on it if you need to, and accept the challenge to see things differently when you can tell it is taking you farther down the path to healing.

65

Be selective who you share with.

Telling anyone who will listen is obviously not a good idea. You never know how people will respond to your story and it can end up becoming another hurdle when they respond in a nonsupportive way. Especially at first, be very selective about whom you share your personal story or challenge with, but find the right supportive people and mentors who get what you are going through and will offer empathy and strength.

66

Read books that uplift and inspire.

Feed your mind with positive books, music, and entertainment that give you strength and light. Bringing dark themes and negative influences into your mind is detrimental. You are taking an active part in overcoming something difficult which requires extra effort, so surround yourself with uplifting things that inspire growth.

67

Develop your tools for moving forward.

As you visit with your support groups, therapists and others who have gone through what you have experienced, take note of the books, processes and other things that helped them and that you connect with. Develop your bank of tools, so to speak, of what helps you move forward, then continually utilize them.

68

Give yourself time to find footing.

Everything takes time, and everyone is on a journey of personal growth, continually progressing. If the abuse or adversity happened recently, you may still feel shaky. Breathe in, use the tools in this book and those you are taking in from others. Move forward with intention. Trust and believe that inner strength and feeling more secure will come; give it time. You will find your footing.

69

Use processes that you learn consistently.

Avoid stopping the processes before they become habits. Keep building on your progress and keep moving forward. There are ups and downs in life and you will experience the same through this trial. The processes and tools you are utilizing will help you get back up. As you apply these processes they will become habits. You will add to each one, building healthy habits that keep your mindset and inner strength intact.

70

Right people will appear when needed.

You will be amazed at how the right people at the right time will show up to help you in your time of need. Keep the faith; you are not forgotten and there is plenty of strength to lean on in your weaker moments. Most people are generous and kind. Believe it and attract that goodness to you. You will be that for someone else too as you overcome and push through this trial.

Set and Achieve Goals on Purpose

71

Visualize desired result and the outcome.

Visualize yourself at the end, achieving the goal. Get that image clear in your mind. Think of all the things you will be doing and experiencing and see yourself reaching that goal. Feel what it feels like to achieve it. If you decide it is going to happen and put action to the thoughts, you will do the very things required to bring about your desired result and make it a reality.

72

See what it takes to achieve.

If you know all the steps required, great. If not, research and study it out. Talk to other people who have accomplished what you want to accomplish and ask them what they had to do to achieve it. Read stories of people reaching the same goal and glean from their wisdom and experience.

73

Break goals down into three actions.

When you know what you need to work on and the actions you need to take, be wise about the starting point and break it down into the first three actions. It may take more actions than three, but beginning with three actions is less overwhelming than taking on all the tasks at once. You will continue the process, building on each achievement until you have reached your goal.

74

Three ways to complete three actions.

With each of the three actions you come up with, break them down into three ways you can achieve each action. For example, if you are going for a promotion and one thing you need is more sales, your action would be: "increase sales," and your ways would be: (1) call leads, (2) set up appointments, and (3) follow up. With increased focus on how to achieve each action, you have a plan you can work on.

75

Can't change past, only moving forward.

What you focus on EXPANDS. There is nothing you can do about the past, so you can stop thinking about that right away. Past setbacks and failures are in the past, there is no sense in revisiting them and dwelling on the negative. You learned what you have learned from them, now put your focus and energy on moving forward. Hope comes when you focus on what can be and what you are working toward.

76

Forgive yourself for your past setbacks

Forgive yourself for past mistakes and setbacks so you can move on. Realize that you are not perfect, no one is, and failure is not final until you stop getting back up. Forgiving yourself is sometimes the hardest thing to do, but it brings renewal and more hope in your soul and provides a positive way to move forward. You are worth multiple second chances.

77

Believe in yourself, see yourself accomplishing.

If your mind can see it and you believe you can do it, then you will. Firm belief in yourself is more than half the battle; it is everything. Believe you can do it and you will figure out how to because you will have the strength and determination. As you build on that belief which fuels your passion, you start seeing yourself accomplishing your goal, which makes it a possibility.

78

If you get off track, reassess.

As you are working toward your goals, you may get off track or notice it isn't working. Don't sweat it, reassess what is not working and think it through. You will see what needs changing and you will have your new starting point with that action. The key is to keep moving forward, trying out all the ways you can to accomplish your goal. Persistence will get you there, never give up!

79

Celebrate the achievement when it's complete.

Take time to own your accomplishment and celebrate your achievement, even the little victories along the way to reaching the end goal. Seeing what you achieved adds to your confidence and positive self-image. It helps you move forward, facing the ups and downs, building on each achievement and the personal growth it brings. This continues to build your inner strength.

80

Reach your goals. Set some more.

Now that you have accomplished your goal, keep going forward. You are becoming the person you envisioned and developing your talents. Your weaknesses are beginning to become strengths as you work on them. Keep going, keep building, reach high and know your worth. Don't stop believing and achieving!

Be Comfortable with Success--Own It!

81

Allow yourself a new peaceful lifestyle.

Think about the new lifestyle you are creating and embrace the peaceful feeling it brings to your soul. Allow yourself a new way of living that is not tied to the negative feelings of the past. Embrace the way it feels when things are working out and you are achieving your goals.

82

Avoid traps of old belief systems.

Old belief systems may creep back in and try to stop your progress. Be vigilant to not let them take hold. Use your positive affirmations and keep the vision of your desired outcome. See what you have already achieved and accomplished by applying yourself. Build on your strengths you have discovered and the talents you are developing. Protect your thoughts; they activate behavior.

83

Adjust to new feeling without chaos.

Sometimes people cling to what is comfortable. If you have been in crisis for long periods of time you might be more used to feeling unrest. Take in the peaceful feeling that comes from all your hard work of forgiving and moving forward intentionally. You will get used to the way it feels without chaos and even be able to bounce back better from any down days that might come.

84

Expect good things coming your way.

What you put out there and how you see things creates your reality. Expect the good in the world that is coming your way and invite more of it. Stay in the positive mode that sees the possibilities of a fulfilled, peaceful, successful life.

85

Claim and take in the accolades.

Be present, and take in the accolades and pats on the back that you are getting. It is a sign of good self-confidence and maturity when you can appreciate your success. You can do this in a way that is not puffed up or self serving, rather appreciating your hard work, and being O.K. with the praise. You will find the place where you are comfortable with success.

86

Life is what you make it.

You are making your life better by intentional living, reprogramming beliefs, forgiving, and putting your goals into action. Keep moving forward and build the life you want for yourself and your prosperity. Keep moving forward, carving out your best life one decision at a time. Believe you are worth it ...YOU ARE!

87

Continue to learn and be educated.

Keep your mind active and engaged in learning. It furthers your development, makes you and life more interesting and improves your general outlook. Whether it is a degree, certificate or continued education for your job, you'll be glad that you are dedicated to learning because it advances you in more ways than one.

88

Show others how to treat you.

When you have a healthy self-image and carry yourself with confidence, people in general will respond with respect. If they do not respond or treat you with respect, stay centered with your inner strength and pay attention to your boundaries around people you have continual contact with. Avoid saying negative things about yourself and don't play small to make others feel more comfortable.

89

Gain a healthy respect for yourself.

Part of owning your success is having a healthy respect for yourself. Also, attaining more successes will contribute to your self-respect and positive self-image. Respecting yourself is important for many reasons, such as attracting the right partner and friends who will respect you and treat you well. Self-respect guides your attitude and brings positive things into your life.

90

Think big and live to achieve.

Thinking big means to focus your thoughts on your big ideas and desires, and on what you want to achieve in life. Stretch your dreams to be even bigger. Build your way there by putting things in motion through your daily actions, and living to achieve your dreams. Conceive it in your mind, even have it become a part of you, then it begins to come to fruition.

Give Back to Community and Others

91

Priorities: put loved ones first always.

The more you grow, accomplish and achieve, you will naturally want to give back and help others do the same. Setting priorities will keep your immediate and extended family, as well as close friends, as your highest priorities. Giving back to them is so fulfilling because most likely these are the very people who supported you in the tough times.

92

Living less selfishly is a blessing.

Being selfLESS is a blessing because you are enriching the lives of others and your own life is enriched as well. Your focus and intentions are for the other person, but something natural happens--when you help others, you yourself grow too. You will notice the warm feeling you get in your heart when you think of someone else and serve them. It is fulfilling to give, but depleting to be selfish.

93

Donate items instead of throwing away.

Another great way to serve others and give back is to donate. You may have items that are gently used and still functioning, but you are no longer using them. They can be a huge blessing and benefit to someone else. Repurposing goods is always more useful and generous. Thinking of others is a sign of the abundance mentality you are creating.

94

Many hands make the work lighter.

When more people volunteer and work together it creates synergy and projects are completed in a timelier manner. It adds to the sense of community and uplifts everyone's spirits. Your church or community may ask for help with projects in town or for a family--be quick to join in.

95

When you are hurting, reach out.

Sometimes the best way to get over a bad day or week is to find a way to help someone else out. Reaching out can get you out of your own head and release some of the heavy feelings you might be experiencing. It switches the focus to something productive and worthwhile. You clear out the darkness that might be coming back in by actively doing a good deed.

96

Give service to those who serve.

Take time to reach out to first responders and people you know who are actively serving others. They really appreciate it because they know the value of service and it is so uplifting to see their reaction when they are on the receiving end. You may know a caretaker who expends all their energy helping others who you can reach out to and uplift.

97

Improve community through outreach volunteer opportunities.

Improving where you live gives you pride in your community and fellowship with your neighbors. Look for opportunities to clean up parks, pick up litter along the roads, remove graffiti, or meet any other needs in your community. You will be recognized as a leader when you pitch in and you will build relationships with like-minded people.

98

See a need, try to accommodate.

Giving back and serving others gives your life depth and meaning. When you see a need, try to accommodate it. Whether it is giving up a seat on a crowded bus for a pregnant woman or elderly person, or paying the difference at a checkout line for the person who is short on cash and can't cover the amount. Pay it forward and see how good it feels.

99

Gifted with greater capacity for compassion.

Because of your unique trials and the pain you have experienced and come through, you may find you have an increased compassion for other people. What a gift to share the strength you have acquired from facing the pain and moving forward in a positive way! You can authentically speak to certain trials and give hope to others who face similar situations.

100

Share your wisdom and give encouragement.

The wisdom you have gained from working all these *Forward Principles* will help you be even stronger when facing the new trials that may come your way. Even more, you are equipped with empathy, experiences to share about making it through, and the ability to truly encourage other people. "Those who bring sunshine into the lives of others cannot keep it from themselves." --James M Barrie

Contact Me

I would love to hear from you; please share your story with me. It would be an honor to work with you, encouraging and supporting you through the *Forward Principles*.

I do speaking engagements for women's groups, church groups, domestic violence groups, abuse support groups, and at retreats. I also do workshops with small groups, which include one-on-one time with each participant to set goals and individual healing paths.

You are worthy and important, let's press forward and see what possibilities are out there for you, turning your pain into purpose.

Raeann@ForwardPrinciples.com
ForwardPrinciples.com
PO Box 662, Mukilteo, WA 98275

Twitter: @raeannhall
Facebook: @forwardprinciples
Instagram: @forwardprinc

References

Mary Tyler Moore quote from BrainyQuote.com

Robert Frost quote: from the poem *A Servant to Servants*, published in the collection *North of Boston*, 1914

Charlie "Tremendous" Jones quote: from the book, *Life is Tremendous: Enthusiasm Makes the Difference*, published by Executive Books, 1968.

James M. Barrie quote from BrainyQuote.com

About the Six-Word Lessons Series

Legend has it that Ernest Hemingway was challenged to write a story using only - six words. He responded with the story, "For sale: baby shoes, never worn." The story tickles the imagination. Why were the shoes never worn? The answers are left up to the reader's imagination.

This style of writing has a number of aliases: postcard fiction, flash fiction, and micro fiction. Lonnie Pacelli was introduced to this concept in 2009 by a friend, and started thinking about how this extreme brevity could apply to today's communication culture of text messages, tweets and Facebook posts. He wrote the first book, *Six-Word Lessons for Project Managers*, then started helping other authors write and publish their own books in the series.

The books all have six-word chapters with six-word lesson titles, each followed by a one-page description. They can be written by entrepreneurs who want to promote their businesses, or anyone with a message to share.

See the entire Six-Word Lessons Series at 6wordlessons.com